REBELS & SOBELS

A Soldier's Diary of January 6th 1999

BY FRANCIS K. KOROMA

outskirts
press

Outskirts Press, Inc.
http://www.outskirtspress.com

ISBN: 978-1-9772-3498-8

Outskirts Press and the "OP" logo are trademarks belonging to Outskirts Press, Inc.

PRINTED IN THE UNITED STATES OF AMERICA

Table of Contents

How It All Started

The civil war that started on the twenty-third of March 1991 was an effort by the Revolutionary United Front (RUF) to overthrow the then government of Sierra Leone. The RUF was led by Foday Sankoh who had supports from Charles Taylor of the National Patriotic Front of Liberia (NPFL). Major General Momoh had been handed power six years earlier by President Siaka Stevens and a new constitution for a multiparty system was adopted. At the time of the RUF incursion into the borders of Sierra Leone, the army had sent a battalion to Liberia to support the West African Peace keeping Force commonly known as ECOMOG. The army only had a few thousand soldiers and was ill-equipped to control the situation militarily. Foday Sankoh was the leader of RUF and he was not interested in peace talks that early and the battle lines had been drawn.

Six months into the RUF incursion I found myself among hundreds of youths in trucks heading for the Benguma Training Center (BTC) at Waterloo, which was part of the largest recruitment drive in the history of the Sierra Leone Armed Forces. Over 1,000 recruiting tickets has been distributed by family members and politicians to would-be recruits and I had ticket number 200. I had just taken my Ordinary Level exam and I had no idea what I wanted to do, and the idea of joining the army was very appealing even though the war was getting intensified in the Eastern region of the country.

We were joyous; we believed in the cause of fighting off the rebels at all cost. That evening up to 1,500 recruits arrived in BTC, and we were singing this chorus: *"Den wanya den go sabi we, den waya, den wanya aye, den wanya den go sabi we tiday."* To simply put it, we were saying that the rebels would know that day who we were, and many would sing that song to their death at the frontlines.

After a week at BTC, we were divided into three groups: recruits with tickets number 0001 to 500 would stay in BTC, 501 to 1000 would go to Teko Barracks in Makeni, and the rest were taken to Lungi barracks. After about nine to eleven weeks of training we were ready to be sent to various frontlines. One of the recruits once told me he had overhead someone saying the recruits would not be going to the frontlines but rather would be stationed in the barracks left by the older and more seasoned soldiers who were presently in Liberia and in the frontlines in the South and East of the country. I giggled and told him to stop smoking whatever he was smoking, because what he had just said was not realistic at that time.

One Saturday evening we heard what sounded like trucks heading for the barracks and one of the trainers/instructors shouted, "Hey! The trucks are here to take you guys to the fronts." We had only been in training for a few weeks and many of the recruits were in shock at the mention of deployment to the frontlines. We would later realize it was a hoax and we all laughed about it later at the billets. Another big rumor we heard then was that all of us would be given passes to see our families before deployment, but that never materialized either.

The National Provisional Ruling Council (NPRC) Coup of 1992

A few months after completing our basic training at the three training locations, many have been sent to the frontlines and a few of us were at other units conducting further technical or specialized skills training. I was fortunate to be among the twelve soldiers selected to be trained as radio operator at the then Sierra Leone Signal Squadron (SLSS).

During the time when we were being trained to be radio operators, we were billeted in one of the buildings at Wilberforce barracks. That building would be our accommodation for about four to five months. My late brother (Doc) lived about fifteen minutes from there, and I would often spend time at his residence where I would eat better food and watch TV. One night, I decided I was going to play a prank on my colleagues, who were chatting in the dark of the night in the billet. Up till now I did not know how many of them were in there or who was there, but I knew there were people there because of the sound coming from the open bay where we had our mattresses spread on the floors. I had just come from my brother's place, and as I got close to the door I had my weapon at a ready position.

I worked slowly into the dark; I pushed the door unnoticed, finger on the trigger, not knowing that the weapon was at "fire." I jumped and shouted "rebels" and that was followed by the burst of a few rounds from my weapon. I had forgotten a basic weapon-handling technique. At basic training, we were taught to have our weapons on "safe" at all times except if you had to fire that weapon. I failed to ensure that my weapon was at safe prior to the prank, and to my astonishment, I thought I had killed a few of my colleagues. There was commotion and I sprinted out of the building and dashed into the dark. I was scared, afraid, and confused. I cleared my weapon and detach my magazine and placed it on "safe."

There were no cell phones those days and I could not call to confirm what had happened. The best way to find out was to go to the Signal Headquarters where our classes were being held and get news of what had happened. I walked slowly and stood behind one of the windows and listened, but I could not get what they were saying. Fortunately, I saw one of our colleagues (Bah) and I pretended not to know what was had just happened. "Aye Bah! What just happened?" I enquired. Bah then told me that someone had entered our billet and opened fire on some of our colleagues. 'Was anyone hurt'? I asked. "fortunately not," he affirmed. At that moment I felt at ease knowing how closely I had come to shooting dead or wounding some of my buddies. That was a secret I kept for over twenty-five years, and I thought I had to share it for those who were in that room that night that I was the culprit.

Prior to the coup, Captain Strasser had earlier came to the radio room at Cockrill to communicate to some of his buddies who I believed were the same group that attacked the capital a few weeks later. I had worked at the radio room the previous night prior to the coup, and we were told to report to Wilberforce Barracks the following morning. I could not understand why I had to be there because I was looking forward to going home and have some sleep, but in the military, you obey and ask questions later.

On arrival at the Signal Squadron at Wilberforce Barracks few of our colleagues were in formation and one late Brigadier Thoronka came and stated that we should all be ready for whatever was to come without saying what it was. We later learned that some soldiers had abducted the radio that was the only means of connecting other formations and units in Freetown. The soldiers were in a truck that had an antiaircraft weapon mounted on it and were heading for the capital Freetown. That would be same group that attacked the state house that led to the Strasser coup of 1992. As soon as the shooting started in central Freetown, Brigadier Thoronka came and mobilized all the soldiers who were there at Signals that morning. The instruction was that a platoon would join Lieutenant AB Tarawallie, who later became the aidde-camp to Strasser, to counter the coup and the second group would lay an ambush at hill court to stop them from getting into Wilberforce Barrack and its localities. I was with the group that would later lay an ambush at Hill Cut junction.

We left our location in a single file to our ambush position, and I felt like we were being led like sheep to the slaughterhouse. The coup plotters were armed and most of these guys had been in the frontlines for months while freshly graduated soldiers with no actual combat experience were asked to counter the coup plotters with AK-47s holding thirty rounds each.

We moved slowly, quietly, not knowing what would become of us once we encountered the coup plotters face-to-face. We selected our ambush position at hill court overlooking the city of Freetown. We could see smoke and hear the sounds of gunfire and it was frightening. We must have been at our ambush for about three hours when we heard the sounds of trucks ascending the hills below us. News had reached the leadership at the army headquarters that the coup plotters had a white cloth tied to their uniforms; the ambush team was therefore asked to have blue pieces of cloth tied to our uniforms to differentiate ourselves from the coup plotters.

The corporal who was the ambush commander warned us not to fire on the convoy, and I was happy to learn that we were not going to engage the group. We could have been killed because they were armed with rocket propelled grenades (RPGs), and antiaircraft twin barrels mounted on trucks. We came out of our ambush position and walked toward a petrol station where we met some of the soldiers who had attacked the State House. They were having food and drink, and alcohol from the store. Some of them asked us why we had blue pieces of cloth tied to our uniforms, and they warned us to remove the cloth or they would treat us as enemies. No need for argument, and we hastily complied with their instructions.

I knew some of the soldiers from Wilberforce Barracks, and some of them were schoolmates, and I was happy to see some of the guys I did basic training with. The days that followed the coup were marked by looting, commandeering of vehicles, and a total collapse of discipline as many soldiers abandoned their units and positions to join the fun in Freetown. That was the end of the All Peoples Congress (APC) hold on power. A new sheriff, the National Provisional Ruling Council (NPRC) had just arrived.

The newly elected coup plotters sent messages to all the frontline battalions and those of us in Freetown to cease all movement except if they were on duty. The warning was for all service personnel to return back to their previous positions, reducing the looting and chaos that had gripped the capital for over twenty-four hours. I received orders to report to Youyi building at the agricultural department that had heard communications between rebel commanders on one of their radio frequencies. I would report there at 8:00 a.m. and return home at 4:30 p.m., and my job was to listen and note all radio communications between RUF and NPRC of Liberia. In the summer of 1992, I was among a battalion of Sierra Leone contingent headed to Liberia.

ECOMOG

I was one of the radio operators of the third contingent aka. Leobatt III, and we arrived in Monrovia on May 12, 1994. The war on our border was not getting any better, and the army was still involved in fighting the war in Liberia. It was time for the Sierra Leone contingent in Liberia to be replaced by our battalion. I was one of the radio operators attached to the Sierra Leone contingent (Leobatt III) to replace Leobatt II. Though the risk was high, the idea of getting dollars was an appealing one, especially for some of us teenagers in our late teens who had just left high or secondary school.

I told my relatives that I would be going to Liberia, and my mom was scared and she started crying. The following day, she came and told me that she had seen a soothsayer, and she was told that I would be OK, and I would return safe from Liberia.

Two weeks later, we were crammed onto a small Chinese Gun boat and headed for the capital, Monrovia. It was a rough night, and a few of us were throwing up and I was seasick. Everyone in the boat knew what lay ahead of us, and a few could be heard praying as we neared Free Port in Monrovia, Liberia. A platoon was deployed at Mount Barclay, the road leading to Gbanga, the strong hold of Charles Taylor's National Patriotic Front of Liberia (NPFL).

We got there early in the morning and I located a half-burnt brick house and I mounted my antennas and established communication to our headquarters in Monrovia. A week later, a platoon of Nigerian soldiers would reinforce us, and we became band of brothers.

One morning we heard a loud sound, and everyone was back into their trenches waiting for instructions. I sent a situation report at our headquarters in Monrovia, but we later heard a cry from the bushes. A Liberian civilian had stepped on a mine and had lost a leg; he crawled to our location and was taken to Monrovia for treatment.

Those days in Liberia, alcohol was merely a means to an end; we had nowhere to go and we would therefore visit all the bars in Monrovia before curfew at 7:00 p.m. One fateful evening, myself and a friend known as MP Jimmy (RIP) arrived in one of the popular bars in Monrovia known as Las Vegas in Freeport. We got into a heated argument with an individual who was in civilian dress, but me and Jimmy were in uniform, and so were the majority of the people in the bar. MP Jimmy was bent on teaching that individual a lesson for challenging him.

Those days, Liberian residents were often dealt with for challenging ECOMOG, even for asking a simple question. There was a scuffle between the two and I had wanted to help my battle buddy, so I joined in the fight. We gave the guy a good beating, but we would later find out that we had just beaten a Nigerian captain who happened to be in civilian clothes.

There had been history of troubles between Nigerian and Sierra Leone troops in the past. One Corporal Koroma was shot in the head at that same bar, and a Sierra Leone soldier had also shot a Nigerian soldier to death a few months later, which many of us took to be a revenge for Corporal Koroma's death. Word got around to the nearest Nigerian checkpoint that one of their officers had been seriously beaten by two Sierra Leone soldiers. A local guy at the bar advised us to run for our lives because a section of Nigerian soldiers were on their way to the bar.

We got sobered little bit and we took off running and got a taxi and asked the driver to take us to our deployment position at Ops Mount

Barclay. The taxi driver would not take us there because he would be late to make it home because of the 7:00 p.m. curfew. MP Jimmy knew someone at 72nd and we decided to go there and pass the night.

We got there and I sat at in a corner of the parlor whilst MP Jimmy was talking with a female friend in one of the rooms. I took out my revolver, which I had bought at a checkpoint for $50 and pointed it at my temple. The alcohol was getting hold of me at that moment and I thought I could take out the revolver and play around with it. I had the revolver pointed at my right temple and wanted to pull trigger. It was not that I had wanted to commit a suicide, but I thought that the revolver was at "safe." I was about to pull the trigger when a little girl about the age of four to five years ran and stood about six feet from me and gazed at what I was about to do. She took off running to a door on my left and I pointed the revolver at her direction and pulled the trigger. Boom!

I had just missed killing a child, but the child had also saved my life, I believed that she was an angel sent by God to save my life. I dropped the revolver on the floor; MP Jimmy and the female ran to see what had just happened. I told Jimmy not to worry about it. "It was an accidental discharge," I said. I took the magazine out and cleared the weapon and placed it at safe. I had wanted to tell MP Jimmy what had happened that evening two years later, but I could not because MP Jimmy had passed. He was a great friend and we shared many memories in Liberia, may his soul rest in peace.

Six month later, I was sent back to the Headquarters in Freeport, Monrovia, but later got deployed to Bo Waterside (Liberian-Sierra Leone Border). Fighting had intensified between Ulimo K and Ulimo J in that part of the country. Our mission was to keep the two factions away from each other, but the situation got worse. The fighting was mostly tribal, between the Khran ethnic group and the Mandigo tribe. I could remember one of the Khran fighters kept looking at me saying, *"Da meh da Mandingo meh."* The reason was because I had Koroma sown on top right corner of my camouflage, and most Koromas spelled Khroma in Liberia are of the Mandigo tribe.

We were cut off from the rest of Liberia for a while, and we could not go across to Sierra Leone because the RUF rebels were right there at the border with Liberia. I later returned to Monrovia, and that trip was a difficult one because one of the civilian vehicles had earlier in the week been ambushed and one of our soldiers by the name of Corporal Sesay was shot point blank in front of the civilians. I read all the Surahs I could read and every Bible verse I could remember because I was traveling in a commercial vehicle that could be stopped and searched by the rebels. I had been selected for an interview at our headquarters in Monrovia to become an officer cadet. Two weeks later, I was on my way to Freetown and a month a later in a KLM flight to the United Kingdom to be trained at the Royal Military Academy Sandhurst.

The Royal Military Academy Sandhurst

A few months earlier I had been selected as the only cadet to be trained at the Royal Military Academy Sandhurst where kings, queens, and princes had earlier graduated, and I had no idea what lay ahead of me. I would have to say that I was the most experienced in terms of years of service in the entire intake of three companies, because I had been enlisted for almost five years and I had seen actions prior to my selection to the academy.

My experience at Sandhurst is far the best in my lifetime, where I dined with kings and princes. This academy is the British equivalent of West Point in the United States where wimps need not apply. It has been almost twenty-two years at the time of writing, but the memories are still fresh in my mind. The first few weeks in Sandhurst involved ruthless discipline, a series of kilometers of what we referred to as "yomps." I had just left Liberia, where I was part of the Sierra Leone third contingent (LEOBATT III) to Liberia to complement the Western African peace keeping force (ECOMOG).

My trip to the United Kingdom was the first time I had left the continent of Africa, and I was excited to see the white man's continent. My first nervous experience was my first dinner at the cadet hall, where hundreds of new British cadets, other overseas cadets from the Caribbean Islands, and princes from Qatar, Bahrain, Saudi Arabia and were all seated, murmuring to one another. I stood nervously and scanned the whole group; one of the cadets I saw I thought might have come from Africa, and to my astonishment I was glad when he told me he was from Ghana. We bonded immediately, and we never separated after that evening until twelve months later when we graduated. It was that same day that OJ Simpson was acquitted because I had listened to few British cadets moaning about the outcome of the proceedings. I asked one of the cadets who OJ Simpson was. He looked at me for a second and said, "Don't worry, mate."

Sandhurst can be hell, especially for the faint of heart, and if you have any doubt about this then go and ask His Royal Highness Prince Azim, son of the Sultan of Bruni, who quit the academy after only two weeks, and many others who never matched across old college after twelve months of training and I am proud to be one of those who made it to the end. There was sleep deprivation, and during every exercise you would be digging shell scrapes or trenches depending on the duration of the exercise. The academy has trained leaders from Europe, kings in the Middle East, and coup leaders mostly from the continent of Africa. The first five weeks of training are renowned for being one of the toughest experiences most people will ever go through. Having lived it, I would agree with that assertion.

I became one of the most hated in my platoon some days, mostly the British cadets, for a simple opinion I had on leadership: "Leaders are born not made." It is a belief I still hold up to this day. The whole issue is debatable, and I totally believe that great leaders can be born or made but being born is the most mysterious part of leadership in my opinion. I was confronted by a few of the cadets and asked me to explain what I meant, and I told them that the phrase was a no-brainer. The academy prides itself among the best in teaching and prepping up leaders around the globe, and any assertion that leaders are born not made was contrary to the academy's belief and a slap in their face by a cadet from the tiny country of Sierra Leone.

After our first three months at the old college, we were allowed out of the academy for the first time. We spent that weekend moving our stuff to the new college. For those cadets who were relegated, they had to stay at the old college and continue with the next incoming cadets who would be starting their military carrier. The following weekend, a few of us from overseas, referred to as overseas cadets, decided we would visit London. An officer cadet from Jamaica asked us to accompany him to Seven Sisters a subdistrict of Tottenham, North London.

We were all kitted in the academy blazers and headed for the nearest train station in Surrey, and we arrived London in the afternoon. We later decided that we would have to visit Chinatown, a red-light district in Central London. We agreed we would go to a strip club in West End, unaware of the financial burden we were getting ourselves into. We were young, inexperienced, and most of us had just started life. We each paid five pounds sterling at the door and we were greeted by some gorgeous ladies, who took us to our seat. They wanted us to be in different seats, but we kicked against that. We told them what we wanted, and we were served by those ladies, and we knew the cost of the drinks, but we were not told other added costs.

I had decided I would spend only twenty pounds sterling: five at the gate and fifteen for drinks. At my third drink, I asked the lady who was serving me to bring my bill. I surveyed the bill like an infantry officer conducting a map reading or land navigation. I saw forty-five pounds, and I asked her whether that was for two people. She smiled and said, "No sweetheart, that's yours." "Sweetheart, forty-five pounds?" "Yes," she acknowledged. At that moment, I started sweating and felt uneasy. I whispered to the Ghanaian cadet to ask for his bill, and he had taken more drinks than I had. His reaction was hilarious, "Charlay! Seventy-eight pounds!" We did not have credit cards and they were only accepting cash. Two of the bodyguards escorted us in pairs to an ATM for cash withdrawal. Everyone felt sober as soon as they discovered what their bills were. We took the last train from Liverpool to Surrey; we sat quietly in one corner gazing at each other. We laughed about it the following weeks, but it was not funny when it happened.

We became friends and we started going out every weekend, but we never repeated what happened in our first outing. Our group comprised of myself from Sierra Leone, Wortodzor from Ghana, Patience Medi from Malawi, Reid from Jamaica, MacLean from Trinidad, and Sebesta from Swaziland. We would always eat in a group, and the supervisor at the cafeteria would always come to our table and ask us if we would like to have more food.

The academy's alcohol policy was that no cadet from the academy must be seen within three miles from academy consuming alcohol in any pubs. One weekend, we decided we were going to take a chance and consume alcohol at one of the pubs. That was the wrong idea. A sergeant major from another company noticed us and decided to have a seat with us. We were nervous at his presence, but he cheered us to continue drinking. He was Welsh man and we each bought him a glass of Lager. We were happy that he did not bring up the policy, so we all went back to our barracks laughing about it.

On Monday morning I saw my sergeant major at our classroom, and I knew something was wrong.

"Officer Cadet Koroma."

"Yes, Sergeant Major."

"Come with me please, sir."

We were always referred to as "sirs" by all enlisted ranks. The Ghanaian cadet and I were marched to the company commander's office because the rest of the other cadets were in different companies. We were given a red book that contained the policies and regulations pertaining to the academy. We were asked if we would like to seek legal counsel, but answered "no." We were reprimanded for two weeks and prohibited from leaving the academy; we had to be in a "barracks dress" with a white belt and had to pick up trash around the academy for two weeks.

At 9:00 p.m., we would have to be in our class A dress for inspection every night. Almost two nights before we finished our punishment, I was about to be late because I had run out of polish to clean my boots. I decided that I would use a Vaseline to shine my boots that night. Hahaha, that was a fun night because the event that ensued would have to be left for another day.

We came to know each other, protected each other, helped each other out. Officer cadet Patience Medi from Malawi was the only one who did not graduate with us. He was relegated to another term and we all paid him farewell at the end our term at the academy. During one of our dinner nights, a British colonel had sat with us at the table and greeted each one of us. He was anxious to know where we had each come from, and he would later refer to us as Africa's future coup plotters and rebel leaders, a compliment I did not like at the time. To some extent he was right—there had been several Sandhurst graduates who were notorious coup plotters in the continent. Johnny Paul Koroma and my first cousin Major Abdul Mansa-Kama Koroma were all Sandhurst graduates who were later executed by the Tejan Kabbah because of the AFRC coup of 1998.

My worst experience came in December of 1995 when I was taken out of the exercise because I was almost frozen out in the snow close to where I was lying on guard. It had snowed for hours and hours and the trenches were wet and cold, and I could hardly grab my weapon or speak. I was scheduled to pull guard from 12:00 a.m. to 2:00 a.m. and at this time I could not feel my feet, and I was totally losing all my other senses. At that moment, my memory was drawn back to patrols in Liberia. There was one patrol I kept reviewing in my head, and that was when I went on patrol closer to the rubber plantations after the Firestone massacres of civilians by the National Patriotic Front of Liberia. I had an infantry radio on my back and armed with an American-made Uzi rifle 22LR. The patrol was made up of a platoon of Sierra Leone contingent, with about two sections of Nigerians who brought along an armored personnel carrier (APC) commanded by one captain Victor, and ours was led by a captain P.S Koroma. As we got deep into vacated farmlands, you could sense that these places had not been inhabited in a long time.

I continued revisiting other occasions in my mind and I must have "frozen to death" at that moment. The next thing I felt were other

British cadets trying to warm me up, and others were getting me tea to drink. I was taken to a tent where other overseas cadets had already been taken and were waiting to be lifted to the academy for immediate medical treatment due to frostbite. The healing from that frostbite took a toll on me, and I came back to the academy after Christmas holidays from London in crutches.

I had gained weight, and I was left with no money, reasonably, because I had not received the stipend the Sierra Leone government sent me. I felt abandoned, had lost interest, and did not want to be there. Two weeks later, the academy assisted me with some cash from the academy fund, and I could not understand why no one back home cared much about my situation. I returned home in September of 1997. Many of my friends and some family members could not understand why I had to come back. "You should have stayed there," someone said, but I wanted to be in the military. I have dreamed of being a general one day.

The war in Sierra Leone was still raging and things had really worsened since I left. The NPRC regime was no longer there and a new government was now in place. The Sierra Leone People's Party (SLPP) government, especially the then minister of defense, a former military man himself, did not like the army for reasons best known to him. The army had several fighting with the Kamajors in the east and south of the country. The Kamjors were local hunters mainly from the Mende tribe and mostly from the south and southeast of the country. Many in the army believed that the government was using the Kamajors as a proxy force and the SLPP government by the help of Hinga Norman was arming the Kamajors at all cost at the detriment of the national army. A few army officers had been locked up at Pademba Road; their crime was fighting back against Kamajor attacks on their locations.

In November of 1997, I was sitting with some of my soldiers of my platoon and we heard what sounded like gunfire coming from the Mile 91 town center. We grabbed our weapons and ran toward the sound of the gunfire, and we met some civilians running toward our direction. They told us that the Kamajors were harassing some people at the town center and they had shot a man. I instructed the soldier carrying the Rocket Propelled Grenade (RPG) to aim high and shoot. He did and the entire place was quiet; we moved tactically to the town center and to our astonishment they had left the town. My battalion commander at Camp Charlie wanted to know what the issue was, and I sent a situation report in the morning. I left that position early December of 1997, and a week later the Kamajors attacked the location, where they killed one of the soldiers that I knew well. He was a popular soldier who used to carry a radio with him everywhere he went, and I had warned him about not playing the radio at night for fear of revealing his location.

Lack of Discipline

One would have to agree that lack of discipline in the army was what led to a second military coup in less than a decade. George Washington once said that "discipline is the soul of an army." In essence, the Sierra Leone Army had lost its soul and could not therefore prosecute the war. The two major political parties were responsible for the demise of the army. They failed to support the army in all aspects: poor housing, poor recruitments, and no strategy in retention. Junior noncommissioned officers (NCOs) were randomly selected from battleline battalions and commissioned. They were referred to as "field commissioned officers" and some of them lacked the necessary tools required to be a military officer. There were no requirements but brevity and some of them lacked the basic education and therefore lacked confidence.

Being an army officer means being able to lead morally, have integrity, and have a sense of purpose. These field commissioned officers were not taught principles of war, and they did not know what it means to manage men. Man management is an important aspect of military leadership; it means allowing your men adequate time to rest when there is not much going on, so they can be fresh for challenges ahead. In as much as those field commissioned officers added numbers to our ranks, they created a vacuum whereby the military was void of seasoned NCOs to train the new soldiers. Some of those field commissioned officers spent time with their platoons and sometimes consumed alcohol and smoked marijuana together. That brought about familiarity, and soldiers were therefore morally corrupted by officers who were supposed to lead them.

Every officer at the time had what we used to call "bat men." The role of a "bat man" was not defined, but could range from taking an officer's loot home to buying alcohol for the officer and mostly were used to get the officer a "morale booster" (woman) for pleasure. Marijuana was issued to soldiers for consumption by the government in power, and a soldier who is under the influence of such a substance could be less effective in the face of an enemy. As the war continued, the officer corps started losing control of their men, and the government could not rely on the military to prosecute the war, and therefore resulted to asking foreign armies for help. We had the Gurkhas, the Executive Outcome from South Africa, the Nigerians, and Guineans. Nigerians and Guineans made up the bulk of foreign troops helping the regular army against the RUF. That lack of discipline and leadership within the ranks led to another coup of 1998 by lower ranks of the Sierra Leone Army.

Three Badges of Honor

I am proud to have served three armed forces: the Sierra Leone Armed forces, the British Armed forces, and the United States military, respectively. Each of these military branches are unique in their own ways, and I would not have exchanged anything else for the opportunities they afforded me. All these militaries are responsible for making me who I am today. The Sierra Leone military is modeled in a British style and all formations and drills, rank structure, and insignias are similar. The United States military, on the other hand, is totally different from these two militaries. A platoon in the U.S. Army would consist of more men, and I found it interesting that each of their platoons would have staff sergeants, sergeant first class, and a few lower ranks such as privates, private first class, specialists, or corporals. A platoon in the U.S. Army is often commanded by a second or First Lieutenant and a staff sergeant or Sergeant First class as a platoon Sergeant. A British platoon is often commanded by a lieutenant or sometimes a second lieutenant and a staff sergeant as a platoon sergeant. I have often been asked by folks, mostly from the U.S. side of the house, questions such as: which army is the best? I have deliberately not given a whitewashed answer to that. "Best" is a relative term and it depends on who you are to. During my time in Britain, the British always saw themself to be the best military in the world. Rightly so, the United States military can also say the same. My perspective though is different because I have served both militaries, and I would have to say that both are unique, similar, and different in other ways.

One major difference is that the U.S. military often refers to what it calls "mission first." It is rather paradoxical that "mission first" is then followed by "people always." The British Army, on the other hand, had something similar to the American military's "mission first" mentality. It was called the "main effort."

For instance, during a mission a platoon commander would be tasked to carry out a particular action that needed to be achieved as part of the company commander's overall intent. "The main effort" would then become so important that no matter the conditions of the men, it must be carried out. However, when I was at the academy in Sandhurst, "main effort" was then focused primarily on the men and women who would carry out the mission rather than the action of doing so.

Another major difference is what I would refer to as their doctrines. The United States military believes in overwhelming firepower. They would prefer to have a better ratio to that of the enemy and their doctrines are that of what I would refer to as concentration of force—more men, and more equipment to defeat an inferior force. The British Army's doctrine is based on the notion that a well-trained, smaller unit of men can defeat a larger inferior force and so therefore their doctrine is referred to as "economy of force." The ability of both militaries to cater to their service members is well beyond excellent.

Rebels or Sobels

In the military, discipline is what keeps it going and without it there would be no military. Suffice to say that discipline within the ranks and file of the military was at its lowest during the war. The military had great supports from the entire population for many years, and close to the end of the NPRC regime. The Revolutionary United Front had gained some popularity in the southeast of the country, but that could not be said of the military. Soon, some civilians started labelling the military as "Sobels." A Sobel was a term used to describe an insurgent in military uniform. RUF resorted to killing and maiming civilians wherever they went. There were folks especially, in the suburbs, who believed that some of the attacks were carried out by military personnel. The insurgents had military uniforms and carried similar rifles, and it was difficult for civilians to understand the difference between the two.

What was also true was that there were a few bad apples in the military whose tactics were not different from the insurgents. Psychological warfare is an important aspect in military operations. The military had not done well to convince the population that they had the will to prosecute the war. The population had lost trust in the army, and therefore anyone in military uniform was a Sobel. It was not a fair description and it was an insult to every service member or family members who had lost loved ones due to the senseless war. The military hospital was full with wounded soldiers from both Liberia and from frontlines in the southeast of the country. The military cemetery at Lumley was getting full with soldiers killed in both wars.

There were several missing pieces here; we had the national army, the Kamajors, the Executive Outcomes from South Africa, and other civil defense forces depending on which parts of the country you were from. The three main players in the war were the national army, the Kamajors, and the RUF. As the population continue to view the army as Sobels, we started seeing local hunters morphing from hunters to paramilitaries. As the war dragged on, the army had to contend with two enemies: the RUF and the Kamajors. RUF was happy to see the national army fighting it out with the Kamajors. This allowed them to recruit, regroup, and launch fresh attacks against our deployment locations with minimum ease. Importantly, the army too had lost trust with the Tejan Kabbah's administration. His minister of defense Chief Hinga Norman was the architect of the Kamajors. He was a former military man himself, but his hatred of the military was hard to understand. I had refused to render a salute to him when he visited our location a few weeks after we had kicked out the insurgents from the capital. I had a platoon of Nigerian and Sierra Leone soldiers under my command at No.1 Christ Church in Central Freetown. Chief Hinga Norman single handedly ensured that any military officer who had hands in fighting back against the Kamajors was locked up at the famous Pademba Road Prison in Freetown. Many service members had seen that to be a betrayal of their service and they had lost trust in the people they were asked to protect.

The AFRC Coup

The majority of the enlisted soldiers who pulled off that notorious coup in 1998 against the Sierra Leone Peoples Party (SLPP) were members of the Sierra Leone Armed Forces football team. Abu Zagalo, Adams, and others made up the armed forces football team, including three commissioned officers: myself, Lt. AB Sesay and Lt. Kargbo aka Testing. Prior to my arrival to join the armed forces football team, I was deployed at Mile 91 where I was the platoon commander and our headquarters was at Camp Charlie, about a twenty-minutes drive from the town of Mile 91. That was my first platoon after I came from the Royal military Academy Sandhurst in the United Kingdom.

I was at Cockerill in Freetown trying to lobby to get parts of the stipend I was supposed to have received during my training at Sandhurst. One major aka "Property" saw me, and he motioned me to see him immediately. He said: "We have not met before, what is your name, junior officer"? I answered: "Second Lieutenant Kassim Koroma." Mile 9 was under RUF threats, and several ambushes had taken place for weeks by the Revolution United Front (RUF) rebels. There was an ambush a week earlier that claimed the life of a friend I knew back during our days in ECOMOG in Liberia; his name was Shekuba. He was crushed when one of the vehicles that was involved in the ambush rolled over him. Major Koroma aka Property wanted two junior officers to reinforce Mile 91, and I was his first catch. The second junior officer would then later be one Lieutenant T Yamba, who'd had altercation with some police officers in Kono a few weeks earlier.

We left Freetown early in the morning sometime in October of 1997, we reached Mile Siaka in the afternoon. We were asked to take restroom breaks, drinks, and food before our final leg to Camp Charlie. Mile 91 was hot at that time, not only from the RUF but the Kamajors as well. There was a breakdown of confidence between the Tejan Kabbah government and the military. There was no trust on both sides and the AFRC coup was no surprise to many service personnel. Soldiers were being killed by Kamajors and nothing was being done, but many officers and other ranks who dared to fight back against the Kamajors had been taken to Pademba Road Prison. The Tejan Kabbah government had created a proxy army to challenge the constitutional army by the help of a former Sierra Leone army officer by the name of Hinga Norman. Hinga Norman loathed the army so much that he was ready to replace the army with the Kamajors.

Johnny Paul Koroma, who later became the leader of the Armed Forces Revolutionary Council (AFRC) met me at Mile 91 a few months earlier, prior to his arrest in Freetown. We sat together and discussed lengthily about the Royal Military Academy Sandhurst, where he had graduated years back. He promised to speak with Staff Officer 1 Operations (SO1 OPS) to have me transferred to his battalion where he was the commander at OPS Moyamba. A few days later he was arrested in Freetown and taken to Pademba Road Prison due to a planned coup according to the government.

I later received orders after Christmas to join up with the rest of the armed football team, and I was happy to be back in Freetown. A majority of the AFRC coup plotters were enlisted or other ranks who made up 90 percent of the Armed Forces football team. Abu Zagalo and Kabbah "China" were the coaches. The enlisted soldiers of the team were billeted at Wilberforce barracks where they planned and executed the coup. We had just played a competitive match at Mountain Court a weekend before the coup, and not one of the commissioned officers was aware of their plot. When we learned of who the coup plotters were, we were astonished. That coup was not a sophisticated one compared to the NPRC coup, and I can categorically state that the AFRC coup would not have been successful against the previous APC government.

The army at this moment was very disgruntled, because many soldiers believed at the time that the government was favoring the Kamajors over the national army. During the morning of the coup, one Major Jopp, the commander of the British training team, met me at the Wilberforce Officers' Mess (Canteen) and asked me what we were going to do about reversing the coup. I shrugged and said: "I wish I knew, sir." The Army Chief of Staff Brig Hassan Conteh had promised Tejan Kabbah that the situation would be taken care of.

Later, the Russian-made MI 24 helicopter gunship was in the air, and most of us thought that it was there to suppress the coup but that never happened. The coup plotters resulted to arresting most senior officers of the Sierra Leone Army for what they referred to as lack of support from those officers and several other political appointees who were still in Freetown. Many residents and foreign nationals sought safety at the Mammy Yoko Hotel in the West of Freetown. Tejan Kabbah was not willing to go quietly and he had asked his then friend General Sani Abacha of Nigeria to help him root out AFRC regime.

Tejan Kabbah installed a propaganda radio station at Lungi that would send information about the defunct government and AFRC respectively. Many Nigerian soldiers were arrested and taken to the officers' Mess at Wilberforce Barracks but were later released on the order of Major Johnny Paul Koroma. AFRC attacked the Mammy Yoko Hotel, which they believed housed many of the politicians, but they were driven back. There was a British special forces guy who was armed with a general-purpose machine gun (GPMG) and he was deployed at the roof top of the hotel. He would open fire on anyone who would attempt to attack the hotel, but he later left when the MI 24 helicopter gun ship opened fire on the roof of the hotel. The pilot of that gun would later face a court martial board but was vindicated.

Former NPRC strong man Captain SAJ Musa had arrived from the United Kingdom to join the AFRC regime. Tamba Brima aka Gulitt was admitted at the 34 military hospital, and I had gone there to see how he was feeling.

Those were the early days of their administration and ECOWAS was still debating whether the AFRC should be removed from power militarily. I sat and listened to SAJ Musa and Tamba Brima as they discussed what strategies they had to take to prevent foreign intervention. I rudely interrupted them and advised them that any plans to prevent foreign intervention would have to include securing the airport. There were Nigerian troops at the airport and Jui respectively. I bluntly told both men that they had no chance of holding onto power with Nigerian troops at the airport, but they were not interested, so I waved goodbye and good luck. I saw Tamba Brima once after that officers' mess but I never met SAJ Musa again. These men were like brothers to me, we grew up together at Wilberforce Barracks and Tamba Brima was my age group, may their souls rest in peace.

It's been almost a decade since RUF attacked the shores of Sierra Leone; their aim was to seize power in Freetown. They were able to achieve that without firing a single shot when AFRC invited the rebel group to form a coalition against the deposed SLPP administration and ECOMOG. It was an unbelievable sight for many Freetownians when they finally saw the devil in a plain sight. RUF had killed thousands of people and displaced over a million. Johnny Paul Koroma had calculated that bringing the rebels out of the jungle would finally bring peace to Sierra Leone and lengthen his hold on power. RUF had other ideas, and they were not shy to state boldly on a few occasions that they would eventually kick both ECOMOG and AFRC from power.

AFRC representatives had skirmishes with RUF fighters in Freetown on a few occasions that I could remember. One evening I was awakened up by what seemed like a gunshot at the officers' mess in Wilberforce Barracks. I got out of my room and went toward where the commotion was taking place. Someone then said to me, "Hey Kassim, go back, there is a problem between AFRC and RUF." There were a few more gunshots then there were screeching tires and the area was once again quiet. An RUF strongman known as "Super Man" made the officers' Mess his residential home. Him and his RUF fighters occupied the mess and emptied the entire alcohol content that was there for the regular army during normal times.

Tamba Brima aka Gullit had arrested a few senior officers a few days into their takeover of power from the SLPP government. My office at the communication unit was a stone's throw to the officers' mess. One of my soldiers had come to me to report of the arrest of senior officers by AFRC, and I decided to go there and see things myself. I could not believe that soldiers of lower ranks such as privates and corporals were sitting at the officers' mess with weapons aimed at the senior officers ranging from major to colonel, respectively.

I asked one of the soldiers who had authorized them into the officers' mess, and he answered, "Gullit, sir." Gullit was a former primary school mate; we grew up together at Wilberforce Barracks, and his dad was a cobbler at the main guardroom of the first infantry battalion where my dad was once the regimental sergeant major (RSM). I met him outside and we had a chat about the situation, and he wanted me to know that he was going to execute the senior officers for their failure to support their cause. He also stressed that those senior officers were responsible for the plights of our fathers, who the SLPP government had retired out of the military with no benefits after over thirty years of service. I made it clear to Gullit that the plights of our parents were not the responsibility of those senior officers but politicians of both the APC and SLPP parties. He looked at me for a few seconds and said, "OK brother go and get them out of here before I change my mind."

I ran hastily inside the officers' mess and told the senior officers to grab transportation and go home. They dashed out and disappeared into the thin air. As months went by, the relationship between AFRC and RUF started to wind down. I received a work order at my office one morning, and it was interesting to know who the recipient was. The Lines NCO, RSM Kargbo had come to my office and stated that the State House had authorized the telephone department of the unit to have a landline telephone installed at RUF's General Sam Bockarie aka General Mosquito's residence. General Mosquito was RUF's field commander and second in command to then leader Foday Sankoh. I wanted to see the man himself face-to-face, and I decided that I would go with the technicians to his residence at OAU Village.

We got there and unfortunately, a woman at the door answered, "Master is not at home." I assumed she was one of his concubines, and we installed the phone and left without seeing General Mosquito. As AFRC was preparing its forces to kick ECOMOG out, RUF had other plans. RUF must have gotten information about ECOMOG's imminent attack of Freetown because they had left two days earlier, prior to ECOMOG's attack of Freetown to kick AFRC out from power. The majority of Sierra Leone Troops were in the suburbs or their deployment positions prior to the coup. AFRC had barely enough troops to challenge ECOMOG in Freetown, and the RUF fighters had abandon their positions in Freetown and fled back to the southeast of the country. There were stories of killings of regular Sierra Leonean troops by RUF who made it to the jungle with them. Once ECOMOG started its push in Freetown, it was a matter of *when* and not *if* they would achieve their objective. AFRC had threatened to burn the entire Freetown if ECOMOG attack their positions in Freetown, and thanks to God, they never had that opportunity.

My spouse

Trainees at the BTC in 1991

Troop Commander British Territorial Army

Author's graduation photo at Sandhurst

Some members of SLESAO

Author's two year old son in 1999

Map showing distance from Makeni to Rokupr

Author's wedding day

Author in the United Army

First Chairman of SLESAO and current chairman L-R :
Retired CPT Ken Josiah and Retired Major Sylvester Kailey

Intelligence Gathering

As AFRC started getting a foothold on power, they wanted to gather enough information on the ECOMOG troops, mainly on the Nigerians stationed at Jui camp, Lungi, and Kenema. There were two Nigerian nationals who were interpreting every conversation that ECOMOG (Nigerians) were discussing. Everything pertaining to operations and even personal conversations were noted and passed to the higher command. After Lt. Banja joined Johnny Paul Koroma at the State House, I was appointed the new communication officer "Control." My job was to provide a comprehensive analysis on electronic communication that included but was not limited to monitoring and reporting on enemy (ECOMOG) plans, including their movements, deployments, and logistics.

To achieve all these, we relied heavily on the two Nigerian nationals who were willingly or unwillingly available to interpret every discussion on the radios used by the Nigerian troops. Our radio operators were smart enough to locate every frequency used by the Nigerian troops. We had the frequencies of all the Nigerian positions in Kenema and Jui respectively. One afternoon we got information that the then ECOMOG commander General Kobe was to visit his troops in Jui camp, and this camp is the closest of the ECOMOG position to the capital Freetown. That information was passed on quickly to the 120mm mortar crew led by Lt. Bangs. General Kobe did visit his troops and Lt. Bangs and his crew engaged the helicopter that brought General Kobe to Jui. General Kobe was reported to have been wounded from a shrapnel from that assault. General Kobe would later attest to this by saying that: "Whosoever was dropping those mortar bombs was accurate."

I had my reservations about the two Nigerian nationals and I called one of them to my office one afternoon and told him, "I appreciate your efforts, but I want to let you know that I have other Nigerian informants that are listening to what you are listening to. I have been comparing the information I am getting from you two to theirs, and there seems to be major differences." I told him that passing on wrong information would be tantamount to treason. It was a psychological ploy on my side, and he assured me that whatever information they were giving me was true to the best of their knowledge. A few days before ECOMOG invaded Freetown, the two men never showed up. I went to their respective locations to pick them up and they were nowhere to be seen. They would later be arrested by ECOMOG troops and taken to Jui after AFRC's withdrawal from Freetown.

ECOWAS had scheduled a meeting between AFRC and Tejan Kabbah for a peaceful resolution. Both parties were not forthright with those arrangements. Tejan Kabbah wanted AFRC gone by any means whilst AFRC had wanted to stay in power at all cost. ECOMOG started bringing in reinforcements of heavy artillery and more infantry battalions. During this time, AFRC had started building a makeshift airfield a few miles outside of Magburaka in Northern Sierra Leone. The Lungi International Airport was already in the hands of ECOMOG and AFRC desperately needed somewhere they could have their cargos dropped off at a location unknown to ECOMOG at the cover darkness. One evening, the makeshift airfield was busy with activities. A fixed-wing aircraft landed that evening carrying one Major Fonty Kanu and other top brass such as Major VL King and the then chief of Army Staff Colonel SO Williams. The origin and nationalities of the pilots were unknown but believed to be Ukrainians. The occasion was

a test drive by AFRC for future operations, but that never came to frui-
tion. The aircraft had brought ammunition; however, that ammunition was found to be the wrong munitions they were expecting. A few
minutes after the plane had left, an ECOMOG Alfa jet was seen flying
above the vicinity and the makeshift airfield was vacated immediately.

Operation Sunset

We were sitting outside what is now JCU at Wilberforce Barracks and I heard what sounded like a mortar round far off. I tried to check on all the other radio stations to confirm their status: "All stations, all stations, this is Control, over," "All stations, all stations, this is Control, over." I was not getting any responses at that moment because all the handheld radios we were using had been jammed. The entire radio network had been jammed and all conversations to and from were distorted and inaudible. I went to the main radio room and tried to use the main radios that used Morse code, but we had the same issues.

At that moment I realized things were getting out of hand, because communication is an important aspect of war and the Nigerian troops had just taken the initiative in the electronic warfare. We didn't have cell phones, Facebook, or WhatsApp then, so we relied heavily on land lines to pass information. I made a few calls to the army headquarters at Cockerill about what was going on. It was no more a secret at that moment because the Nigerian troops were on the move to Freetown on two fronts. The propaganda radio station in Lungi used by ECOMOG and the Tejan Kabbah administration was asking residents in Freetown to resist the Junta. The radio station was even passing on false information by stating that Wilberforce Barracks and other units had been captured by ECOMOGS troop.

It was all part of ECOMOG's psychological operations to dislodge the Junta. The AFRC Junta was not a popular one, and most of us were happy to see them go but the army got dragged into it because the entire Sierra Leone military was then regarded as the Junta by both ECOMOG and the Tejan Kabbah administration. A few weeks earlier, the Nigerian troops in Kenema had been heavily beaten by the Sierra Leonean troops in Kenema and many of their soldiers had been wounded or killed and the rest had walked through the jungle to seek solace in Guinea. All the Nigerian positions in Kenema, Jui, and the Lungi international airport had come under attack by AFRC. At the same time, the Nigerians were able to sustain Lungi airport and flew more battalions from Nigeria to replenish their positions. The Jui camp came under the most attacks because of its proximity to the 120mm Chinese mortars positioned around the hills.

On the second day of the assault, every member of the Sierra Leone troops stationed in Freetown was asked to reinforce their colleagues. I joined the rest of the troops at the eastern police station in eastern Freetown. I had a platoon and I was tasked to take the left flank that led to the children's hospital and the main force took the main Kissy Road. We had a single formation through Duff Cut Market, and there were many civilians who pretended to be supporting our presence, but I knew that was all false. I stopped and asked some of the civilians if they had noticed any Nigerian presence in their vicinity, and they said no. As we approached the hospital, there was a complete quietness different from where we had seen civilians standing outside. I signaled to the troop to take a knee, and I asked the point man to observe for enemy presence.

A few seconds later there were sounds of gunfire everywhere; we had just been ambushed by the Nigerians who were all but positioned at the hospital waiting for us. It could have been worse if they had allowed us to get into the intersection, but the ambush was not effective in my opinion because many of us were able to withdraw from that ambush and I saw the majority of the men again after we reorganized at the eastern police station. We could not account for about five of the men, and they could have been killed, wounded, or just missing. In the midst of the ambushed I jumped into a gated compound and my watch I had brought from England a year earlier was missing but I was grateful that I was alive. I asked one of the soldiers to follow me to Wilberforce barracks, and I was disappointed to see many of the SLA troops in the street drinking whilst others were in the front fighting.

The following day was the same; ECOMOG kept pushing and the ability to hold Freetown was fading by the day. The AFRC folks were nowhere to be seen, and the army was facing a confidence crisis and probably facing a defeat. The last battle was fought at Hill Stations toward OAU village, and the then chief of staff late General S.O Williams was sitting with a few soldiers at Hill Cut Junctions. The Nigerians were shooting constantly at us from hidden positions as we moved toward their positions. The Nigerian troops were then heavily ambushed when they attempted to push their way through OAU village. A Nigerian lieutenant was killed, and he was beheaded by the AFRC folks, and his decapitated head was taken to Colonel S.O. Williams who was not pleased at the sight of it.

It was getting late, and it was almost 7:00 p.m. when I returned back to Wilberforce Barracks; the communication building was already vacated by many of the soldiers. At this time, ECOMOG had taken most of the city, and there were rumors that AFRC had surrendered. The fact was that almost every member of the regime including their RUF compatriot had left Freetown for the jungle, some to Liberia and others into hiding. I met one of the officers at JCU known as BJ and we stood there alone thinking what to do next, and one senior officer known as Colonel Bash passed us on his way to the officers' mess. BJ said that it would not be safe for us to stay at the building and allow ourselves to be taken prisoners by ECOMOG.

The city was quiet, Wilberforce barracks was calm, there were no gunshots, and many of the soldiers had left the barracks to reorganize and come back. I saw one of the soldiers loitering around the building and I asked him to follow me and his name was Mansaray. Mansaray was believed to be suffering from a mental illness and I was not sure how I was going to manage him with a fully loaded AK-47 in his possession. I told him to sling his weapon and we left for the two-hour walk to Goderich. We were still in uniform and many civilians at that moment had started installing checkpoints. At Lumley, we met a checkpoint manned by civilians and as soon as they saw us they wanted to know who we were. At that moment Mansaray asked me if he could open fire; I asked him not to. They let us through when they realized that we were armed with an AK-47 and a 9mm semiautomatic pistol, a Browning Hi Power made in 1971, in my holster. I would not have hesitated to use it if I had felt that my life was in danger, but they were smart enough not to bother us.

We walked past Juba Barracks, which was also vacated at the moment, and arrived at Goderich at my fiancé's residence at about 11:00 p.m. Her family received me well, and they were happy to learn that I was alive, and Mansaray told me that he would prefer to go to the jungle instead of staying in Freetown and I would not see him again after that night. I would have to say that it was uncomfortable and awkward at first, but I felt at home, and that lady would later become my wife. The next day, ECOMOG reached Goderich and I was there as a civilian watching what was going on. I saw one member of the Sierra Leone Army, and his name was Harleston, with the Nigerian troops.

After two weeks in hiding I decided that I would leave and go home to Wilberforce Barracks to see my relatives, especially my mom, who must have been worried about my whereabouts. I took a taxi to Lumley and we met a checkpoint at Juba Barracks, and everyone was asked to disembark. I had a little scare when a Nigerian soldier I knew back in ECOMOG in Liberia saw me at the checkpoint. "Haha Ogamie, how now? Are you still in the Army?" he asked. At that moment, I held his hand and pulled him to a corner and told him I had left the army a year ago and I did not want anyone in the taxi to know that I was in the military. He understood, and he gave me fifty-thousand leones and that was a lot of money at that time. Many members of the Sierra Leone Army had either left with RUF, or had been arrested and locked up at Pademba road prison. Many had gone into exile in Liberia or

Guinea, had surrendered, or were in hiding for fear of being a prisoner. Many of us had to leave not because we were part of AFRC, but many viewed the military as AFRC, therefore the army could not divorce itself from AFRC.

The Refurbished Sierra Leone Army

Many Sierra Leoneans, especially in the south and east of the country, wanted a new national army. The Kamajors were touted to replace the Sierra Leone Army, and Tejan Kabbah's administration did little to reduce that claim. The Kamajors were instrumental in helping the Nigerians in taking over cities of Bo, Kenema, and Kono. However, the Nigerians had their reservation about the effectiveness of the Kamajors in fighting off the remaining SLAs who were bent on coming back to drive both these forces away for good. The Kamajors relied on mystic powers they believed would protect them from bullets, and that was proven wrong on several occasions when they had altercations with the SLAs both in Bo, Kenema, and in other places where the Kamajors were badly beaten. Tejan Kabbah's administration was determined to "disband" the entire Sierra Leone army when he came back to power after ECOMOG had kicked out AFRC from power.

There were many members of the military who were still locked up at the infamous Pademba Road Prison in Freetown, awaiting trial for several crimes, according to the administration. There were many others locked up in other areas such as Wilberforce Barracks, where I was a prisoner at one time for almost a week before I was released. Hundreds were in what I would refer to as a prison camp at the Benguma Training Center (BTC) at Waterloo about eighteen kilometers from Freetown. After several months of fighting between ECOMOG and the remaining SLAs and RUF alliance, the Nigerians realized that it would almost be impossible to achieve their aim without including the other members of the Sierra Leone Army who were languishing in prisons. All the Sierra Leone Troops who formed part of the Sierra Leone contingent from Liberia were also taken to the notorious Pademba Road Prison. At that time, most of the Kamajors had return to their farms and villages, believing they had succeeded in driving the entire Sierra Leone military to oblivion.

There was a concession that every member of the Sierra Leone military in hiding and those at BTC were to report to Lungi Barracks for consideration for being allowed back into the army. Most of us had not done anything else in our lifetime but military and some of us lacked the necessary skills or tertiary education to cut it in the corporate world. There were hundreds of us who showed up, and the life we lived was not different from a prison camp. We had suddenly become prisoners in our own country, and a foreign army was parading us as criminals and nonentities. There was a mix of all ranks from private to colonel, but respect and military discipline was accorded to all. The officers were concentrated at the former officers' mess and all the enlisted personnel were living in the other quarters of the barracks. I was not a stranger to the vicinity because my dad was at one time the regimental sergeant major (RSM) of that barracks about ten years earlier.

A month later, we were sent to the Benguma Training Center where we were given uniforms, and many of us were happy to be back in uniforms again. Our time at the camp was spent discussing our plights, the administration, ECOMOG, and the war that was going on. Honestly, some of us were hoping that ECOMOG would be kicked out by the folks in the jungle because of the way we were being treated by the politicians and ECOMOG. We had one meal a day that was made up of rice and beans, and the only thing available was what our families loved ones and relatives would bring us goodies such as:

soap, sardines and sanitries. The situation was precarious and many of those family members took the risk of visiting us at the camp and on many occasions were ridiculed when people realized what they were doing at that time.

The major in charge of the camp, one Major Ahmed, was very instrumental in keeping us together at the camp. He was honest, and he would tell us: "Your government in Freetown has abandoned you; they don't want you anymore, and that is the fact." There was a phrase he was well known for: "There is no secret when a woman is about to give birth; her legs have to be wide opened." ECOMOG was in haste to have us sent to the frontlines again to fight against mostly our friends, squad mates, relatives, and sometimes family members who were on the other side. It was a difficult situation but there were not many other options available to us at that time. After we were given uniforms, we were formed into two infantry battalions. One would go to the east in Kono to reinforce ECOMOG and the battalion I was with were to go and reinforce the Nigerian troops in Daru via Kenema.

We were loaded into several trucks and headed for Kenema with only two AK-47s in our possession. We arrived Kenema around 10:00 p.m. at night, and many of the Kenema residents must have thought we were part of the Nigerian troops. We left that night to a school just outside the city, and that would be our destination because our presence caused a lot of commotion when the residents woke up to learn that the visitors the previous night were not ECOMOG but SLAs. The following afternoon, the school was surrounded by Kamajors who started to threaten us to leave town or they would kill all of us. We only had 2 AK-47s compared to over one hundred armed Kamajors. We later learned that they requested for reinforcement from other towns and villages to come take us out of town. Nigerian troops showed up later and asked them to leave, but they were adamant and the Kamajors requested that we leave town, or they would kill us all.

At that moment, the Nigerian officer warned the Kamajors that if they insisted on fighting, "I will arm the SLAs and let you two fight it out here and now." That was not the message the Kamajors were expecting, and they finally started leaving. They threatened that they would be waiting for us in Daru or anywhere else if we decided to stay. The Nigerians must have realized that our presence in Kenema would be counterproductive, and a decision was made to take us to Teko Barracks in the northern city of Makeni in the Northern Province.

We arrived in Makeni, and we did not have to face the amount of resistance we faced in Kenema. After about three weeks of our stay, we were deployed in the northern town of Kalangba and the residents were very happy to receive us. Our counterpart, the other infantry battalion, were already in Kono currently with ECOMOG side by side repelling the insurgents. The battalion headquarter was at Kalangba but got moved to Pendembu together with about 70 percent of the battalion. I was the only officer at that moment at Kalangba with a platoon. We were getting situation reports that AFRC/RUF activities had been on the increase around the Eastern fronts, especially around the diamond-rich city of Kono. The platoon was not enough to defend the town, and I received a reinforcement from Kabala after I had spoken to the battalion commander about it.

Late November of 1998, the insurgents had started attacking positions in all fronts including positions in the Northern Province for the first time since the AFRC regime was kicked out of power. About seven to eight hours prior to the attack of Pendembu by the insurgents, mainly former Sierra Leonean soldiers, two of the officers had arrived Kalangba on their way there. One of the two officers would never make it back alive because he would be later killed in action. Lieutenant MT arrived Kalangba around 6:00 p.m. on his way to Pendembu and I asked him to pass the night at Kalamgba. About 10:00 p.m. that night, we started hearing heavy gunfire from a distance and we assumed that Pendembu must have been attacked. We could not confirm it because we did not have radios at Kalangba, and we would later get the full information around 6:00 a.m. in the morning when I started receiving soldiers from Pendembu.

I grabbed two soldiers from the platoon headquarters and checked all the trenches to ensure that we were ready if we were to be attacked.

About 6:00 a.m. in the morning two officers, Lieutenants ABB and JJ, reached Kalangba and we were very anxious to learn what had happened. They confirmed our suspicion, but we did not know what the status was in terms of the number of casualties. A truck arrived Kalamgba around 11:00 a.m. heading to Pendembu including an armored personnel carrier (APC) carrying some Nigerian troops and they told us that eleven of our men (nine SLAs and two Nigerians) had been killed during the attack. They also confirmed that three SLA officers were among the dead, and that news broke every one of us down. We could not figure out who those three officers were, and it was a waiting game from that moment.

There were nine Sierra Leonean officers at Pendenbu. Lt. Orpee had passed Kalangba headed to Teko Barracks in Makeni reroute to Freetown to collect six months of back log of our salaries. Lt. MT was with me at the time of the attack, and two other officers, ABB and JJ, had reached Kalangba very early in the morning after the attack. That meant only two other officers may be alive out of the remaining five officers at Pendembu. It was very difficult at that moment to think of which officer could be dead or alive, but I overheard one of the Nigerians in the armored car from Teko Barracks that the commander Lieutenant Colonel B. was not among the Kias. That meant any of the remaining officers could be among the three KIAs: Captain Kaloga, Lieutenants B, K, and Big Joe.

A few weeks earlier, we had all been together at Kalangba, eating together, and we would go the river outside the village to take a shower and played like ten-year-old kids. I visited them at Pendembu weeks before the attack, and it was the same day the SLPP government executed the AFRC coup plotters and other several senior officers of Sierra Leone Army, including a female, Major Kula Samba. We were sitting and drinking a local wine brewed from a palm tree, and someone brought a radio for us to listen to the usual BBC News. We were quiet when we started learning of the names of those they had executed, and there was a complete silence. One of the officers had his dad executed and my cousin Major Abdul Masa-kama Koroma was also among those executed and my uncle was still at the Pademba Road and I did not know of his status. There was a Nigerian officer with us at the time and he was very upset with the whole thing. That officer would later die when the truck he was in got ambushed at Okra Hill on his first leave he had to go to Freetown.

At 2:00 p.m. the truck carrying the dead arrived in Kalangba and the scene was unbearable. The three officers killed were loaded last, and I was able to identify Captain Kaloga and Lieutenants ABB and K, respectively. Lieutenant ABB had earlier passed Kalamgba with a female believed to be a companion of Captain Kaloga, and the female was taken away by the insurgents during the attack. That attack was the biggest in terms of the number of officers who were killed in a single attack since the start of the rebel incursion in the early nineties. That attack was followed by several other attacks, especially in the east, which eventually led to the attack of Freetown on the sixth of January 1999. We received intelligence reports that the insurgents were on the double and were planning an all-attacks on our positions during the Christmas season. In mid-December of 1998, the entire battalion was tasked to reinforce Makeni, meaning that Pendembu and Kalanga were totally vacated. The diamond city of Kono had just fallen and the entire troops of ECOMOG and Sierra Leonean troops were on the retreat to the Brigade at Teko Barracks in Makeni.

The Eagle Has Landed

November of 1998 saw the beginning of AFRC's efforts to overturn what they saw as a Nigerian influence in reinstating Ahmed Tejan Kabbah's administration to power. The "Eagle" was a call sign for Captain SAJ Musa, who was leading the operation to capture Freetown. Most parts of the country, especially in the east, south, and the north, had been cleared of rebels and the administration in Freetown thought the rebels were at the end of destruction by the mighty ECOMOG, mostly made of Nigerians and the refurbished Sierra Leone Army. They were totally wrong because AFRC/former SLAs were on the advance and their target was Freetown.

Our new deployment location was at Binkolo, the hometown of a former president General Saidu Momoh. Another platoon was deployed at another village and my platoon was deployed at a small village called Mangoreh. During this time, our colleagues in Kono were on their way to Makeni after they were dislodged by the insurgents. Three days into our new deployment, the insurgents led by retired captain SAJ Musa aka the Eagle attacked Binkolo around 10:00 p.m. SAJ Musa was the vice chairman to Valentine Strasser of the National Provisional Ruling Council (NPRC). There was a lot going on at that moment, and we were at Mangoreh waiting to see what would come of it.

There was no stopping them currently, even though there was deployment between Binkolo Makeni and my locations at Mangoreh. However, Musa's team decided to take another route to Makeni. I had thought about that for a while during the attack of Binkolo, that their next target could possibly be the village manned by another platoon led by Lieutenant AB (Anzo). Why would you risk taking an open road to Makeni and got ambushed or targeted by an Alpha jet? Lieutenant Sesay's position was attacked around 12:00 a.m. and at the moment I knew we would be next. Lt. AB Bock was at Mangoreh with me to reinforce us but when I checked their position no one was there and I decided to bring everyone else into two positions. The first position was the road leading to the village that had just been attacked. We laid corrugated zincs about 50 meters from the stream leading to the village. I situated the second group upstream, leading to a foot path. My first cousin lance corporal Kandeh whose elder brother was executed a few weeks earlier by Tejan Kabbah's government was with me that night. I told him to keep his eyes open.

I went back to the platoon headquarters and laid on a military-type camp bed I had always used from Kalangba. I was listening to the *Voice of America* when I eventually fell asleep. I was woken up by a sound: "Halt, who comes there?" That was followed by a rocket propelled grenade (RPG) blast from whoever the intruder was. We had just been attacked, and the sounds of small gunfire then sporadic RPG blasts were everywhere. The entire village was in turmoil and I had one soldier with me by the name of Arthur. We crawled our way to a cotton tree then to a nearby primary school just outside the village. The insurgents had already overrun the entire village at that moment, and I and Arthur started running toward the school when we received a burst of gunfire coming from the school. We dashed and laid still for a while and the gunfire ceased, and as our eyes got accustomed to the dark we could see what looked like an individual with an object in his hand. After a few minutes he let out some rounds toward our general direction and left. I instructed Arthur to get ready to sprint across the field. We took off running as fast as we could until we reached the end of it.

We spent the night in the bush with several other civilians who had left the village during the attack. At about 3:00 a.m., the attacking force started leaving the village for Teko Barracks, and it took about twenty minutes before the entire group left the village. We positioned ourselves close to the footpath used by the insurgents and we could hear their footsteps and what they were saying as they went past us. We returned to the village around 6:00 a.m. and I started calling out if anyone was around. Five more soldiers came behind the church and we gathered at the center of the village, discussing what would be our next move. We were there up till 10:00 a.m. and I instructed the remaining soldiers to form a single line and walk to the next village where we met with Lieutenant Anzo and another few soldiers. One of his soldiers had been shot in his left foot and he was in serious pain.

We walked slowly toward Binkolo and arrived there around 1:00 p.m. We met the entire battalion and three staff sergeants had been killed the previous night. The three KIAs who were all staff sergeants all belonged to signals, military intelligence, and the military police respectively. We loaded their bodies in trucks and drove to Makeni, including the wounded. We were burying their bodies when Makeni was attacked by the same group that had attacked us the previous night. Two hours later Teko Barracks and Makeni fell in the hands of Musa and his troops, and that episode started our tour to Freetown. The entire contingents of Nigerian troops and SLAs started the longest withdrawal that would take us from Makeni to Freetown via Binkolo, Kamakwe, Fadugu, Kambia, and Rokupr. The highest-ranking person was one Nigerian major by the name of Major Ahmed. The attack on a northern town of Fadugu was the straw that broke the camel's back.

We had arrived at Fadugu with the hope that we would be able to recuperate from days of walking, but how wrong we were. About 11:00 p.m. that night a group of insurgents attacked the town and the only two possible ways out were the road to Kabala or to venture into the river in the dark. I was one of those that ventured into the river in the dark, and the river got to my neck at one instance and I had to let go of the general-purpose machine gun I had carried with me from Makeni into the river. I swam in the dark and I could hear cries especially from female partners of Nigerians soldiers who would carry their female compatriots wherever they were deployed. My personal help Private Lansana was from Fadugu, the very town we had just been booted from, and I never saw or heard from him again after that night. On the third of January 1999, we took some local boats known as *pam-pam* from Rokupr to Lungi Ferry Terminal. There were well over a hundred soldiers, mainly SLAs from both Kono and the battalion from the North, all there waiting to cross to Freetown. Tejan Kabbah's administration must have been informed of our presence across the capital, and we were not surprised when we met trucks at Tagrin in Freetown. We were taken to the national stadium, and that would be our home until January 6.

The Day

We had arrived on the fourth of January at the national stadium, and the group involved soldiers who had withdrawn from Kono in the east and the other battalions in the north. Personally, I was happy to be back in Freetown again, even though the condition of my arrival was not what I was hoping for. Two weeks earlier, the situation was so bad that we had no time to sleep and prepared defensive positions to repel AFRC/RUF attacks. The rebels were gaining ground as Nigerian and Sierra Leone battalions were on the retreat due to intensive rebel incursions on all fronts.

That fateful morning, I had woken up and decided to use the bathroom. At that moment I saw what looked like someone with a red head tie through the window and the person had what looked like an AK-47. We had Nigerian troops manning the gates to the national stadium, so no one would be expecting gunmen in the stadium without a fight. However, that was what had happened because a few minutes later the rebels were all over the national stadium, including the area by the swimming pool where we were situated.

At this moment most of us were already fatigued after days and nights of walking, and the last thing we were looking forward to be another rebel attack, especially in the heart of the capital of Freetown. For many Freetownians, the war was a distant memory, but that reality would be short lived because the war that had ravaged the rural communities of the country for almost a decade had visited the capital and they meant business.

In the dark of night, the rebels had descended the hills of Freetown to lay claim to it. The attackers were former members of the Sierra Leone Army and the rest were youths whose parents or relatives were sons and daughters of former soldiers who had either been killed during the war, locked up at Pademba Road Prison, or could not be accounted for. Freetown was in turmoil; the battleline had been drawn, the chicken had come to roost, and the battle of Freetown had just started.

About twenty minutes later, we had over thirty to fifty armed rebels in our midst and there was nothing we could do about it. Three hundred meters across the bridge, there were some Nigerians and a few other Sierra Leone soldiers who were monitoring the situation. We had members of our group who had gone out to meet the armed group and started chatting, and I was not ready to meet and greet anyone because I was thinking about how I was going to get myself out of the mess. It was obvious that the rebels would soon have a confrontation with the group of soldiers across the Congo cross bridge.

An hour later, our group was reduced as many had either been abducted or left on their own accord. The situation was getting dicey and our safety was no longer guaranteed. Above the skies were Nigerian Alpha jets cycling the area and across the bridge were soldiers who were frantic and confused and we did not know what was happening on the other side. At that moment, most of us were asking ourselves what was going to happen to us; we were trapped between the rebels and our colleagues, who were armed and ready to pounce on the insurgents.

About an hour later we saw a white jeep driving across the bridge by the insurgents, unaware of a small troop of Nigerian soldiers including a few Sierra Leone soldiers; they were not aware of the presence of ECOMOG troops across the Congo Cross bridge. The passengers in the vehicle were met by bursts of small gunfire and eventually blasted by an RPG bomb. Whoever was in that vehicle had met his or her maker in an instant. The vehicle halted to a standstill, and there was a further burst of gunfire and it was all quiet after that. This was all happening right in front of us, and honestly that is something you would see in a Hollywood movie, but we were seeing it in real time.

The troops across the bridge had started shooting at our location at this time, and at one instance blasted an RPG right at the window adjacent to where we were all seated. There was commotion, a dead soldier lying by the swimming pool, and an armed Alpha jet circling our location, ready to dispense its ammunition. We had to decide or risk getting killed or wounded in some fashion. The troops across the Congo Cross bridge must have realized at this moment that the insurgents had left. A few soldiers and commissioned officers had either left on mutual consent with the insurgents or had been taken by force.

After hanging heads to see what to do to get ourselves out of that quagmire, we decided to send one of our own, Sergeant Mezzo, across the bridge with a letter asking ECOMOG to take us out of the death trap. We had soldiers who had sustained gunshot wounds, and a sergeant from Makeni was killed during the process and his body laid to rest near the swimming pool. He had died earlier when the Nigerian Troops across Congo Cross Bridge blasted the swimming pool with an RPG bomb. The pool was not filled with water and many of the guys were able to jump and seek cover from direct fire. At that moment, ECOMOG had brought in armored tanks and more men from across the bridge. Sergeant Metzger was asked to go under the bridge to meet the troops and confirm to the Nigerian troops that the insurgents had left and that we were not armed. Most importantly, we had the wounded who needed medical attention immediately.

Metzger had on a white T-shirt and he took it off and started waving to the troops across the Congo Cross Bridge. They waved him back and agreed to have him met them, but the situation was scary because the Nigerian troops were occasionally taking target shots at our position. Metzger would later recollect that one of the officers he met across the bridge was a major by the name of Ahmed with whom we had earlier withdrew with from Fadugu in the northern region. Metzger braved his way under the bridge and eventually led the Nigerian troops to our location and we were transported to safety to Collegiate Secondary School, which was also a home for some other senior SLA officers at that time.

The Push Back to Retake Freetown from Rebel Hold

January 7, 1999: Freetown was covered in smoke; sounds of rockets and artillery could be heard from the distance. No one knew what was going on in the far east of the capital in places such as Kissy and its immediate environs. I was worried because my two-year-old son was with her grandma in Kissy and I have not heard of their status. Many of the people who would later arrive at the national stadium from that part of the capital would recount rebel atrocities in that part of the city as disastrous.

We were gathered in a large classroom and we were told that Brigadier Kobie who oversaw all military operations in Sierra Leone was to speak to us. From what we had gone through in the past twenty-four hours, I was not expecting any good news from the general. He was calm and spoke softly with a grin on his face, but he was determined to kick the insurgents out of Freetown who were burning houses, raping, and killing at will. He gave a brief description about the situation and one could sense a general in distress.

At the end of his briefing, he said: "Gentlemen, we all know about the situation in the city, and I am asking for those of you who would like to volunteer to kick the rebels out of Freetown. This is your country, and only you can bring sanity to this country, not ECOMOG or the Kamajors but you, the SLAs." At that moment, I thought that would be a great opportunity to get out of that "prison" and be a part of history. Another officer (Sonny) and me, including close to thirty enlisted personnel, volunteered. We were taken to the main facility of the Sierra Leone Army's communication unit where I was the transportation officer as a second lieutenant and later the adjutant (executive officer) In the early days of AFRC.

Two trucks arrived at Collegiate Secondary School and all those who had volunteered to join the main ECOMOG troops were taken to Wilberforce Barracks for further instructions. A Nigerian major called and asked me to go and talk to young men or adults, many of whom were relatives and family members of present or former Sierra Leonean soldiers at the Wilberforce Barracks canteen. He gave me fifty kilograms of white rice to be given to them for feeding.

Many of those I met were friends, schoolmates, and relatives who had been consolidated at that location for fear of them joining the insurgent against ECOMOG. I could sense that almost all of them were happy to see one of their brothers from the security team with them. I told them the reason they were there was not to be hurt or maligned but rather for their accountability and safety. My official residence was also a five-minute walk away and I took the opportunity to go see my mom, who was in a very bad state because she did not know whether I was alive or dead at that moment. She cried when she saw me, and she was sad to learn that I would not be staying but I had just come to say hi. I did not tell her where I was about to go, but I asked her to pray for me and she did. Two hours later, we were loaded into two trucks headed for the capital to drive out the insurgents who had invaded the capital from the hills forty-eight hours earlier.

We got loaded into trucks and headed to Central Freetown where the rebels were causing mayhem at that moment, burning houses and killing residents in the capital of Freetown. I was with a Nigerian Captain who would later be shot that same evening, and another SLA officer Lieutenant Sonie was in another truck and the entire group was a mixture of Nigerian soldiers and Sierra Leonean troops. The Nigerians wanted us to lead since we knew Freetown better, and we had troops on both sides of Siaka Stevens Street advancing toward the Cotton Tree and State House. We had another group advancing from St. John via Pademba Road. The insurgents were still at the State House and they had taken many of their wounded including civilians to the Connaught Hospital. As soon as we reached Connaught Hospital, several of the wounded came out and some Nigerian soldiers deliberately opened fire on some of them. I informed a Nigerian sergeant major to instruct his men not to shoot at unarmed civilians, and his answer was: "Oga, they are all rebels." One of the wounded soldiers from Connaught Hospital was a primary school mate of mine in the eighties and he went by the alias Lolo, and I am not sure if he was shot that afternoon because I have not seen nor heard of him since that fateful afternoon.

We spent some time around the Cotton Tree area due to extreme firepower from the insurgents coming from the State House area. A boy who was almost half naked came running from Pademba Road axis, unaware of our presence, and he was cut down with a machine gun in an instant. Most of the Nigerian soldiers were part of a rein-forcement that had arrived a few days earlier and they were new to their environment and were willing to shoot at anything that moved in front of our advance. The insurgents eventually withdrew, taking their wounded with them to an unknown location and we advanced and stopped at the end of Siaka Stevens Street.

We were searching a corner street close to a mosque and a Nigerian soldier saw one of the youths with a Brazilian football jersey on. He called the young man and asked him where he got the jersey from, and the guy told him the jersey was given to him by one of his friends. The Nigerian soldier was furious, and he claimed that the jersey belonged to him, and he asserted that the young man could have been one of the people that might have broken into his room the other day when the rebels descended on Freetown. Others tried to calm him down, but he shot the youth with the machine he had in his hand.

Many civilians including Lebanese came out and started distributing water, candies, and biscuits. We were still planning our next move when insurgents opened fire and a Nigerian soldier was shot right in is throat and fell a few yards away from me. He laid there gargling until he finally gave up the ghost. A few civilians were caught in the fire including a former female footballer, and I could still remember her lying there, eyes open, and she must have had a fresh haircut by the looks of her hair at the time of dying. The insurgents had an anti-aircraft weapon mounted on a white United Nations pickup van and were letting go of hundreds of rounds in our direction. Some of them had come back from the State House and cut off our withdrawal route. We withdrew through Ecowas Street, a narrow street path that led to where that Nigerian soldier had earlier shot that young man. The street was too narrow to accommodate the number of us who were trying to get back to safety as the rebels had taken the initiative again. We had gone back close to St. John to reinforce and get more ammunition and personnel. There were civilians who were brave to come out and assist us in carrying ammunition as we advanced back to retake Siaka Steven Street.

We got back to the position where we were attacked in the afternoon around 7:00 p.m., and all our wounded or those killed in action had been set on fire. We settled and passed the night at the intersection of Ecowas Sani Abacha Street. The other SLA officer and I would later be tasked to maintain security along the Mountain cut axis until further notice. Our platoon headquarter was at Christ Church Circular Road /Pademba Road intersection. The following day, my colleague asked if we could take a patrol to St. John. He had a family member who lived there at the time and he wanted to make sure she was alive. The situation could have turned out to be brutal because a fresh platoon of Nigerians had been deployed at the St. John junction and they were ready to open fire when they saw us. We took positions but later realized we were on the same side.

I asked a Nigerian major if he could attach some Nigerian troops with us, because our platoon was totally Sierra Leone troops and we wanted that mixture of foreign troops. We would later be reinforced with a platoon of Nigerian troops, and many of those folks were happy because they had no knowledge of Freetown. The following night, a civilian came to our position and reported that they had seen gun men hiding at the notorious Pademba Road Prison. We decided that we would raid that location because the prison was only about a mile from us. We got there and found out that civilians had actually got into the prison at the cover of darkness and started looting food stuff meant for the prisoners, who had all been freed by the rebels a few days earlier when the rebels attacked the prison to free political prisoners.

The days that followed were meted by sporadic rebel attacks on our locations, consistent artillery bombardment on the hills above us to drive away the remnant of the rebels who had descended on the capital on January 6. Freetown was a mere ghost town, especially in the west of the capital near the Siaka Steven Stadium. Our location was where the majority of those would come through, and I was fortunate to see a few of my schoolmates and others I grew up with at Wilberforce and Lungi barracks.

One morning, five gentlemen showed up at our checkpoint; they were shaking, unkempt, and hungry. They were Nigerians soldiers who had been away from their locations in civilian dress and got caught out and got separated from their colleagues when the rebels attacked Freetown. I loaded them to a pickup truck and dropped them off at Wilberforce Barracks, where the majority of the ECOMOG force was stationed at that time.

One evening, I took some of the Nigerian troops to a bar that just got opened a few days earlier and they had started selling alcohol to those who could venture outside their homes. After a few drinks, I asked them if they could accompany me to Kissy Old Road. They looked at me in bewilderment and were interested to know why. I told them that I had a two-year-old son and his whereabouts were not known. They agreed and we left in a pickup truck around 7:00 a.m., and the driver was an ex-police officer (SSD) known as Big Joe. I trusted Big Joe and he was like an older brother to me. The sooner we got to Up-Gun in the far east of the capital, fear gripped us. It was quiet and the movement and sounds were coming from vultures who were having a party on bodies left behind by the rebels.

We disembarked and walked to where my son was staying; there was nobody there except an old man who I though was dead but was playing dead when he felt our presence. I decided to go to where my son's mom was staying, and the sight was something that stayed with me for a very long time. Two of the landlord's sons had been shot together with other tenants. I knew these people when I used to visit that compound six months earlier. I later learned that they were shot by someone by the name of Saidu Kamolai. We left in haste and returned to Central Freetown, and the capital started rebuilding itself again after the horrors of January 6.

Mob Justice

The days that followed AFRC/West Side boys being kicked out of Freetown by ECOMOG and Sierra Leonean troops were dark days. Youth and other vigilantes were searching for "rebels" for revenge. I witnessed several civilians coming to outpost at No.1 West Street by Pademba Road and reporting their neighbors had collaborated with rebels during their short stay in Freetown. On several of those complaints, I used my judgement and asked those complainants to bring proof of their allegations. On some other occasions, we were too late to have intervened as vigilantes took the law into their hands by causing physical harm, and some residents were even killed in the hands of those area vigilantes.

One afternoon, we had a complaint that there was a Junta guy with a weapon in a corner street near St. John close to Pademba Road Prison. We quickly got into a pickup truck and headed there. We reached the location and there was commotion everywhere, and there were some Nigerian troops with their weapons pointed at some of the civilians who had already killed a man whose lifeless body was lying under a mango tree. The deceased had a special security division (SSD) uniform on, and I assumed he was an SSD personnel. I asked some of the locals and I was told that he got mobbed by some of the area boys who took him for a Junta because he could not properly identify who he was. Those were just a few of the mob justices around that area and many of those incidents were reported to my platoon HQ at West Street at the time, though some of those complaints were never investigated because we had other pressing issues at hand.

Trust between residents in the capital was a dodgy one, and even amongst the fighting troops. Some of the Nigerians troops had earlier confessed that they had been briefed by their superiors not to trust the SLAs because of the earlier escalations during the AFRC/ECOMOG battle of Freetown. Honestly, even us, the Sierra Leone troops, had little trust of the Nigerian troops. We believed that the Nigerians only sought our help when they realized they could not take on the AFRC/ RUF alliance by themselves. They had relied on the Kamajors on their initial attack of Freetown by using the Kamajors to engage the Sierra Leone troops in Bo, Kenema, and Kono while they focused their might against the Junta in Freetown. Once AFRC left the capital, most of the Kamajors retuned and occupied those cities held by the regular army and had little interest in going after AFRC/RUF/West Side boys.

The Aftermath

We would take regular patrols along Forah Bay College and other areas along the hills of Freetown and the capital city was finally cleared of the rebels. The city started rebuilding its lost souls, business, and burnt houses. Many of the residents who had left or were in hiding started coming out, and thousands of those who were at the national stadium started going back to their homes, and many were able to lay their loved ones in peace.

For me, that was the end of a chapter, and another chapter of my life started later in the United Kingdom. I requested for study leave; a year later I was asked to come back whilst I was at the middle for my studies. I was promoted to the rank of a captain in my absence, a rank I never wore. I applied to serve in the British Armed Forces, and I was selected as lieutenant straight away because I had graduated from their academy about three years earlier. I served as a troop commander at the 36th Signal Regiment Headquarters and later transferred to a signal unit in Grace, and I left for the United States four years later.

I had promised my wife that I would not join any more militaries— a promised that was never kept. After less than a year in the United States, I met a recruiter and asked him if I could join the United States military. "Yes sir," he answered, and the rest was history. The decision to join the United States military was by far one of the best decisions

I have made, and I am proud to be serving the best military the world has ever seen. Several of my colleagues who had served in the Sierra Leone Army during the war are presently living in many other parts of the world, precisely in Europe and Northern America. We formed what is known as Sierra Leone Ex Service Association Overseas (SLESAO) and we would meet annually in Maryland in the United States for fundraising to help some of our colleagues back home. I have been to Sierra Leone on a few occasions and it is sad to say that many of these folks who fought those brutal wars in both Sierra Leone and Liberia are languishing in street corners of Freetown without homes to sleep in. The wounded are being left to survive on their own, and there is no standard veteran association to help these guys. May the souls of all the Nigerian soldiers, Guineans, and other soldiers of fortune (The Executive Outcomes, Gurkhas, etc.), Sierra Leonean troops, other armed civil militias, and civilians who died defending our Republic and our way of life rest in perfect peace.

CPSIA information can be obtained
at www.ICGtesting.com
Printed in the USA
LVHW010339230221
679524LV00005B/597